THIS
BOOK
BI

G000255871

Name: _____ Age: _____

Favourite player: _____

2023/24

My Predictions	Actual
The Canaries' final position:	
The Canaries' top scorer:	
Championship winners:	
Championship top scorer:	
FA Cup winners:	
EFL Cup winners:	

Contributors: Peter Rogers

A TWOCAN PUBLICATION

©2023. Published by twocan under licence from Norwich City Football Club.

Every effort has been made to ensure the accuracy of information within this publication but the publishers cannot be held responsible for any errors or omissions. Views expressed are those of the authors and do not necessarily represent those of the publishers or the football club. All rights reserved.

ISBN: 978-1-915571-53-3   £10

CONTENTS

THE CHAMPIONSHIP
SQUAD
2023/24

Jack STACEY

3

POSITION: Right-Back   **COUNTRY:** England   **DOB:** 06/04/1996

Jack Stacey signed for Norwich on a free transfer ahead of the 2023/24 season, upon the completion of his contract at Bournemouth.

His previous clubs included Reading, where he had progressed through the academy ranks, and Luton Town, with whom he had won multiple individual accolades and achieved promotion.

His debut came on the opening day of the 2023/24 season as Norwich beat Hull City 2-1 thanks to Adam Idah's injury-time winner.

Grant HANLEY

5

POSITION: Defender   **COUNTRY:** Scotland   **DOB:** 20/11/1991

Club captain Grant Hanley joined Norwich City in 2017, and has made almost 200 appearances for the club.

A serious Achilles injury sustained in the 2-0 win against Blackburn Rovers ended the Scotland international's involvement in the 2022/23 campaign and he spent the early stages of the 2023/24 campaign in rehabilitation for the injury.

Ben
GIBSON
6

POSITION: **Defender**   COUNTRY: **England**   DOB: **15/01/1993**

Initially signed on loan from Burnley in the summer prior to the 2020/21 campaign.

Following the team's Championship title win, and promotion, Gibson then stayed permanently with the club.

Gibson had started his career with his hometown club Middlesbrough at the age of 10, before captaining them in the Premier League.

Borja
SAINZ
7

POSITION: **Midfielder**   COUNTRY: **Spain**   DOB: **21/02/2001**

Norwich City signed attacking midfielder Borja Sainz on a free transfer from Turkish side Giresunspor.

His start to life in England was a difficult one as a training injury in his first week ruled him out for the first few weeks of the season, and supporters will be hoping he has a major role to play throughout 2023/24.

Liam
GIBBS

8

POSITION: Midfielder   **COUNTRY:** England   **DOB:** 16/12/2002

Norwich City signed midfielder Liam Gibbs from rivals Ipswich Town in the 2021 summer transfer window.

Gibbs has since broken through to the first team, and scored the first goal, winning the club's young player of the season award.

He has switched from number 46 to the eight shirt for 2023/24.

Josh
SARGENT

9

POSITION: Striker   **COUNTRY:** USA   **DOB:** 20/01/2000

USA international Josh Sargent was Norwich City's top scorer during the 2022/23 campaign, bagging 13 goals in all competitions, while also getting to represent his country at the FIFA World Cup in Qatar.

Now playing more centrally, Sargent will be hoping that he can better that tally in the current season, now wearing the number nine shirt vacated by Jordan Hugill.

SQUAD

2023/24

Ashley BARNES 10

POSITION: **Striker**   COUNTRY: **England**   DOB: **30/10/1989**

Norwich City's new number 10 Ashley Barnes joined the club from Burnley at the end of the 2022/23 Sky Bet Championship season.

A one-time Austrian Under-20 international, Barnes spent 10 years with the Clarets and played 200 games in the top tier for them. He celebrated his 500th career league game and 100th career league goal in Norwich's 3-1 against Millwall in September.

Adam IDAH 11

POSITION: **Striker**   COUNTRY: **Republic of Ireland**   DOB: **11/01/2001**

Adam Idah started the 2023/24 campaign in dream fashion, scoring a 96th-minute winner in the Canaries' 2-1 win against Hull City on the opening weekend.

He first announced himself on the scene with a hat-trick against Preston North End in the FA Cup and has since become a full international for the Republic of Ireland, scoring his first goal in June 2023 against Gibraltar.

George LONG

12

POSITION: Goalkeeper   **COUNTRY:** England   **DOB:** 05/11/1993

Norwich City signed goalkeeper George Long on a free transfer from Millwall on the same day that Tim Krul departed for Luton Town in August.

Long will challenge Angus Gunn for the number one spot at the club, having already played 250 league games in his career.

Sam McCALLUM

15

POSITION: Left-Back   **COUNTRY:** England   **DOB:** 02/09/2000

Defender Sam McCallum made 19 appearances for the club last season having spent the previous two years on loan at Coventry City and QPR.

He has shown his versatility throughout pre-season ahead of this season, playing both left-back, centre-back and on the wing, scoring a stunning goal against King's Lynn Town in a friendly.

Christian
FASSNACHT

16

POSITION: **Winger**   COUNTRY: **Switzerland**   DOB: **11/11/1993**

Switzerland international Christian Fassnacht signed for the club from BSC Young Boys in July 2023.

He had made 251 appearances for the Swiss side, scoring 75 goals and registering 43 assists. He's also played for his country. His arrival is expected to add extra energy and goal threat to the wide positions.

Gabriel
SARA

17

POSITION: **Midfielder**   COUNTRY: **Brazil**   DOB: **26/06/1999**

Gabriel Sara arrived at Norwich in the summer of 2022 from Brazilian club São Paulo.

His first season with the Canaries ended in him winning the Barry Butler Memorial Trophy as the club's player of the season, in recognition of his playmaking ability and eye for a stunning goal. He will be integral to Norwich's 2023/24 promotion push.

Przemysław PŁACHETA 20

POSITION: **Winger**   COUNTRY: **Poland**   DOB: **23/03/1998**

Last season was a difficult one for 'Przemy', as he spent the first half of the campaign on loan at Birmingham City, making just a handful of appearances before injury cut his temporary move short.

He returned to Norfolk in January to continue his rehab with the club's medical team and, after returning to full fitness, has impressed in pre-season both in attack and defence.

Jacob SØRENSEN 19

POSITION: **Midfielder**   COUNTRY: **Denmark**   DOB: **03/03/1998**

Danish midfielder Jacob Sørensen signed for Norwich City in 2020 from Esbjerg fB.

His versatility has seen him play in every position across the backline as well as at central midfield, which is often viewed as his most natural position. 'Lungi' is known by supporters for his quiet and unassuming nature.

Danny BATTH

21

POSITION: Defender   **COUNTRY:** England   **DOB:** 21/09/1990

Danny Batth joined Norwich City from Sunderland on deadline day following the sale of Andrew Omobamidele to Nottingham Forest.

A product of the Wolverhampton Wanderers Academy, he made his name with the midlands club before joining Stoke City in 2019. He later joined Sunderland on an 18-month contract during which he won their 2022/23 Player of the Season.

Kenny McLEAN

23

POSITION: Midfielder   **COUNTRY:** Scotland   **DOB:** 08/01/1992

Canaries midfielder Kenny McLean has been a mainstay in the side now under three different head coaches, with his combative style adding much needed aggression.

With Grant Hanley injured, McLean has also acted as captain of the side. At the start of the campaign, he had the second most appearances for the club among the current squad, but is due to overtake his international teammate Hanley in the opening few weeks.

Shane DUFFY

24

POSITION: **Defender**   COUNTRY: **Republic of Ireland**   DOB: **01/01/1992**

Shane Duffy was signed by Norwich City on July 1, 2023, as a free transfer following the expiry of his contract at Fulham.

He had previously spent a number of years at Brighton and Hove Albion where he was an integral part of their rise to the Premier League. He's also captained his country, the Republic of Ireland.

Onel HERNÁNDEZ

25

POSITION: **Winger**   COUNTRY: **Cuba**   DOB: **01/02/1993**

Cuban-born winger Onel Hernández signed a new two-year contract ahead of the current season following a string of impressive performances in the second half of last season.

Ever-popular among the Canaries faithful, Hernández reached his 150th game for the club in the very first game of the season against Hull City at Carrow Road.

Marcelino NÚÑEZ

26

POSITION: **Midfielder**   COUNTRY: **Chile**   DOB: **01/03/2000**

Arriving to Norwich City with two Chilean Primera División titles to his name, as well as experience playing in the Copa Libertadores, Marcelino Núñez is the first Chilean to represent the club.

His first season will largely be remembered for his stunning volley against Birmingham City at Carrow Road in February 2023, which went on to win the EFL's goal of the month award.

Jonathan
ROWE
27

POSITION: Winger   **COUNTRY:** England   **DOB:** 30/04/2003

A product of the Norwich City Academy, Jonathan Rowe featured regularly as a sub during the club's last Premier League campaign, but saw his 2022/23 season curtailed by injury.

His 2023/24 got off to a flyer with a goal in each of the opening four games, including a 98th-minute winner against QPR in the Carabao Cup.

Angus
GUNN
28

POSITION: Goalkeeper   **COUNTRY:** Scotland   **DOB:** 22/01/1996

A son of popular former Norwich City goalkeeper Bryan Gunn, Angus first joined the club as a striker in the Under-8s before departing to join Manchester City.

He rejoined on loan for 2017/18, before sealing a permanent transfer back to Carrow Road in June 2021 to challenge for the club's number one position.

THE CHAMPIONSHIP
SQUAD
2023/24

Adam
FORSHAW
29

POSITION: Midfielder   **COUNTRY:** England   **DOB:** 08/10/1991

Former Leeds United man Adam Forshaw signed for Norwich City the same morning of the 4-0 win away at Huddersfield Town in August 2023.

Adding depth to the midfield, Forshaw also comes with experience of three promotions, two from the Championship and one from League One where he also won the competition's Player of the Season during his Brentford days.

Dimitris
GIANNOULIS
30

POSITION: Left-Back   **COUNTRY:** Greece   **DOB:** 17/10/1995

Now going in to his fourth season representing the Canaries, Dimi Giannoulis has been a regular in the left-back position.

A key cog in a PAOK team that won the Greek league and cup double in 2018/19, he has since joined Norwich and been part of a promotion-winning team. He's nailed down the left-back berth ahead of the 2023/24 campaign.

SQUAD

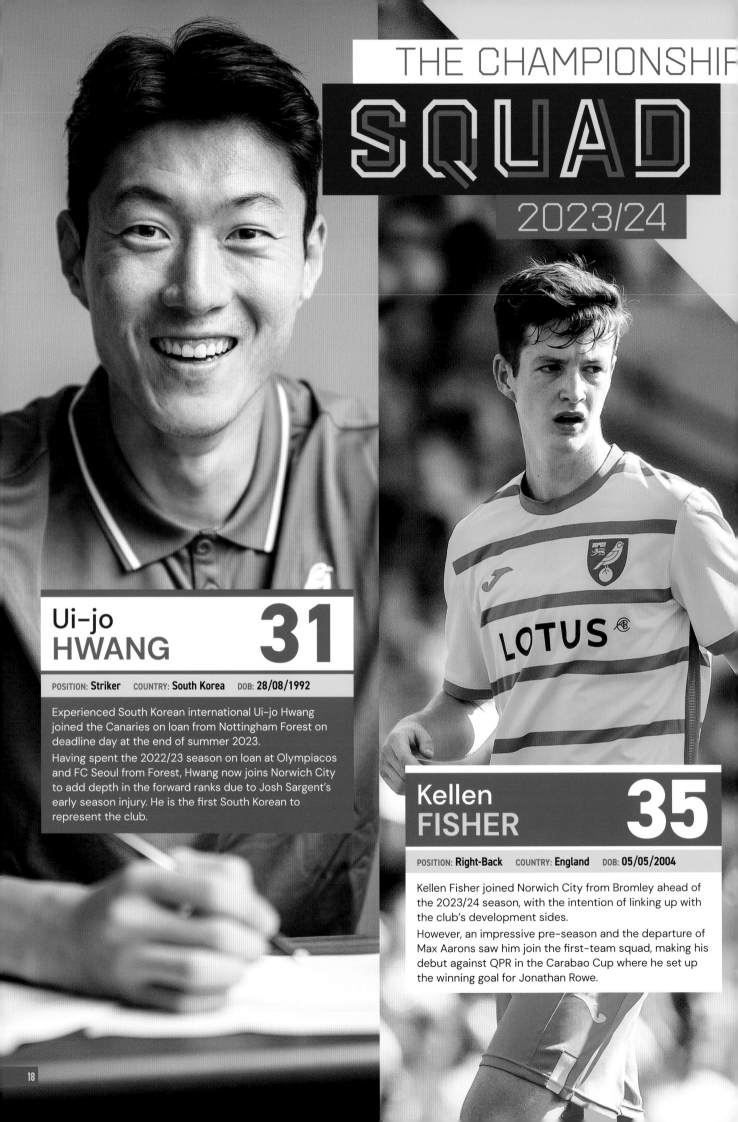

Ui-jo HWANG

31

POSITION: Striker   **COUNTRY:** South Korea   **DOB:** 28/08/1992

Experienced South Korean international Ui-jo Hwang joined the Canaries on loan from Nottingham Forest on deadline day at the end of summer 2023.

Having spent the 2022/23 season on loan at Olympiacos and FC Seoul from Forest, Hwang now joins Norwich City to add depth in the forward ranks due to Josh Sargent's early season injury. He is the first South Korean to represent the club.

Kellen FISHER

35

POSITION: Right-Back   **COUNTRY:** England   **DOB:** 05/05/2004

Kellen Fisher joined Norwich City from Bromley ahead of the 2023/24 season, with the intention of linking up with the club's development sides.

However, an impressive pre-season and the departure of Max Aarons saw him join the first-team squad, making his debut against QPR in the Carabao Cup where he set up the winning goal for Jonathan Rowe.

Daniel
BARDEN

37

POSITION: Goalkeeper   **COUNTRY:** Wales   **DOB:** 02/01/2002

Former Arsenal Academy goalkeeper Dan Barden has had an unfortunate spell of injury and illness over the past couple of years.

He'll be hoping that 2023/24 will offer him the opportunity to get back to more regular playing time, starting with the club's development sides.

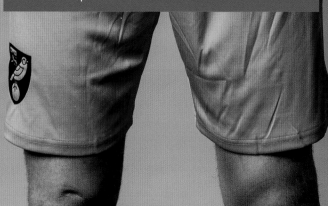

Jon
McCRACKEN

38

POSITION: Goalkeeper   **COUNTRY:** Scotland   **DOB:** 24/05/2000

Goalkeeper Jon McCracken started the season on loan at Scottish Premier League side Dundee.

After four appearances in the opening month of the campaign, McCracken was quickly recalled to bolster the Norwich goalkeeping ranks when Tim Krul's departure to Luton Town was announced.

Vicente REYES

39

POSITION: Goalkeeper   **COUNTRY:** Chile   **DOB:** 19/11/2003

Chilean youth international Vicente Reyes joined the club in the summer of 2023 from Atlanta United 2.

American-born to a Chilean family, he has gone on to represent them at Under-20 level as well being part of Atlanta United's set-up since joining at Under-13 level in 2016.

Tony SPRINGETT

42

POSITION: Winger   **COUNTRY:** Republic of Ireland   **DOB:** 22/09/2002

London-born Tony Springett has been with Norwich City since the age of 12, rising through the ranks to make his first-team debut in May 2022.

After a loan spell at Derby County in the first half of 2023, a positive pre-season prompted head coach David Wagner to include the current Republic of Ireland Under-21 international in his squad for the season.

SPOT...

...THE DIFFERENCE

Can you find the eight differences between these two celebration photos?

ANSWERS ON PAGE 62

21

ONE OF THE HARDEST THINGS TO DO IN FOOTBALL IS TO STICK THE BALL IN THE BACK OF THE NET.

NOT LEAST BECAUSE THERE ARE USUALLY 11 OTHER PLAYERS TRYING TO STOP YOU DOING JUST THAT!

SHOOTING FROM DISTANCE

Good service is obviously important, and a good understanding with your striking partner is also vital, but when it comes to spectacular strikes, practice is the key to hitting a consistently accurate and powerful shot and to developing the timing and power required.

EXERCISE

A small-sided pitch is set up with two 18-yard boxes put together, but the corners of the pitch are cut off as shown in the diagram. There are five players per team, including goalkeepers, but only one player is allowed in the opponent's half.

The aim of the drill is to work a shooting opportunity when you have the ball, with the likely chance being to shoot from outside your opponent's penalty area, from distance. The teams take it in turns to release the ball into play from their own 'keeper - usually by rolling out to an unmarked player.

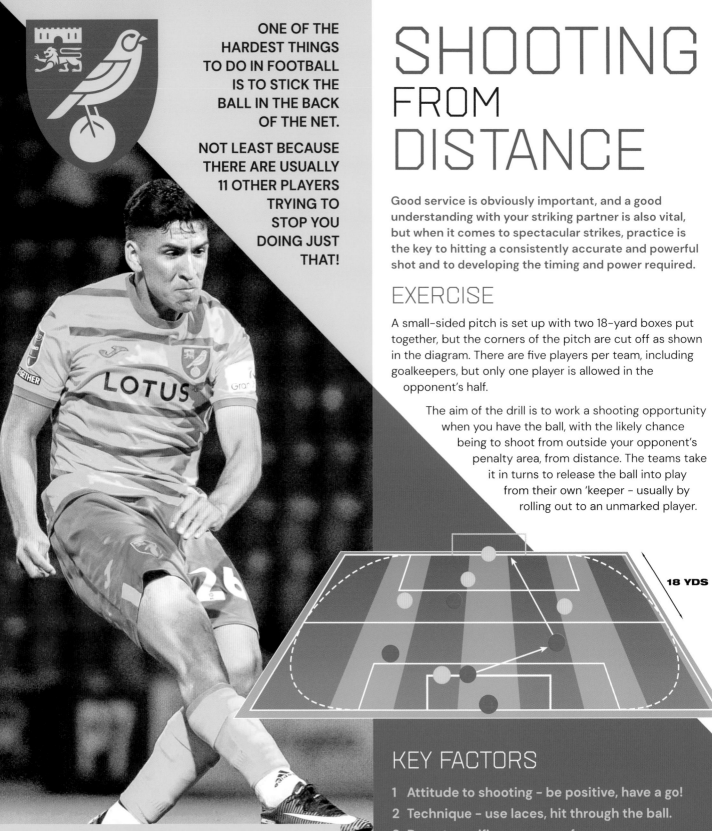

18 YDS

KEY FACTORS

1 Attitude to shooting – be positive, have a go!
2 Technique – use laces, hit through the ball.
3 Do not sacrifice accuracy for power.
4 Wide angle shooting – aim for the far post.
5 Always follow up for rebounds!

SOCCER SKILLS

The size of the pitch can be reduced for younger players, and it should be noted that these junior players should also be practicing with a size 4 or even a size 3 ball, depending on their age.

CHRISTIAN
FASSNACHT

16

23

NORWICH CITY WOMEN

THE SUCCESS OF THE NORWICH CITY WOMEN CONTINUES TO GO FROM STRENGTH TO STRENGTH WITH STRONG INTEREST AND GROWING LEVELS OF PARTICIPATION AT ALL AGE GROUPS.

A great 2022/23 season was capped off as the Norwich women's first team won their seventh Harrod Sport County Cup title after defeating Mulbarton Wanderers in the final.

In front of a Carrow Road crowd of 2,690, goals from Ceri Flye, Katie Knights and Liv Cook saw Norwich run out comfortable winners and then lift the trophy as former head coach Shaun Howes signed off in the best possible way.

With growing numbers of spectators watching the women's team in action at The Nest in their league fixtures, the team played their first FA National Women's League (Division One South East) match at Carrow Road when they took on Ashford Town on Sunday, April 16, 2023.

A highly successful afternoon in the history of Norwich City Women saw the team produce a sensational performance as they won an eight-goal thriller 5–3.

The match attracted an outstanding crowd of 7,585 all of whom went home impressed with the entertainment provided.

THE NORWICH WOMEN ENDED THEIR LEAGUE CAMPAIGN WITH A FOURTH PLACE FINISH IN THE DIVISION ONE SOUTH EAST SECTION OF THE FA NATIONAL WOMEN'S LEAGUE.

With Flo Allen as general manager and Martin Herdman as the new head coach, the 2023/24 campaign will see the City women look to build on the success and progress made last season and continue to climb the leagues in the women's game.

For more information on Norwich City women visit the club's official website www.canaries.co.uk where full details of the Women's team can be found plus information on future fixtures at The Nest and Carrow Road.

As the club's end-of-season awards were presented, Ellie Smith was voted the Norwich City Women Player of the Season.

The 27-year-old midfielder saw goals and assists form a regular part of her matchday performances with Smith also landing a number of Player of the Match accolades during an impressive campaign.

ELLIE SMITH

DAZZLING DEFENDERS

DAVE WATSON, CRAIG FLEMING AND ADAM DRURY WERE ALL OUTSTANDING CANARY DEFENDERS AND CONTINUING THE TRADITION IS CURRENT CAPTAIN GRANT HANLEY.

Craig Fleming was a great Norwich City servant having initially joined the Canaries from Oldham Athletic in June 1997 for a fee of £600,000.

A solid, brave and extremely reliable central defender who was blessed with a great turn of pace, Fleming was voted Player of the Season during the 2003/04 campaign as Norwich City were crowned Nationwide First Division champions and made their long-awaited return to the Premier League.

Forming an excellent central-defensive partnership with Malky Mackay throughout the majority of his Carrow Road career, Fleming's loyalty to the Canary cause was rewarded with a testimonial against Newcastle United in July 2006.

Dave Watson was plucked from Liverpool reserves in 1980 and proved to be one of many shrewd signings by the Canaries in that era.

He played 38 league games in the 1981/82 campaign as he won the first of two promotions while at City. A brave and strong defender with a great ability to read the game – Watson was named City captain in the 1982/83 season and ended the campaign as Player of the Season.

Outstanding club form saw him win his first international cap as England defeated Brazil at the Maracana in June 1984. Watson skippered the Canaries to League Cup glory at Wembley in 1985 and promotion as Second Division champions the following season.

DAVE WATSON

DATE OF BIRTH:	November 20, 1961
PLACE OF BIRTH:	Liverpool
NATIONALITY:	English
NORWICH CITY APPEARANCES:	256
NORWICH CITY GOALS:	15
NORWICH CITY DEBUT:	December 26, 1980

Ipswich Town 2 Norwich City 0 (First Division)

CRAIG FLEMING

DATE OF BIRTH:	October 6, 1971
PLACE OF BIRTH:	Halifax
NATIONALITY:	English
NORWICH CITY APPEARANCES:	382
NORWICH CITY GOALS:	13
NORWICH CITY DEBUT:	August 9, 1997

Norwich City 0 Wolves 2 (Nationwide Division One)

Adam Drury was the captain of the Canaries' 2003/04 Nationwide First Division title-winning side. The long-serving left-back joined Norwich City in March 2001 from Peterborough United.

Signed by Nigel Worthington, Drury went on to enjoy 11 seasons at Carrow Road while playing over 350 games for the club. He was an extremely reliable and consistent defender who excelled in one-on-one situations. His polished performances in 2002/03 saw him voted Player of the Season.

Drury's time at Carrow Road was certainly eventful as he experienced three promotions, two relegations and a play-off final. His loyalty to the Canary cause was rewarded with a testimonial match against Scottish giants Celtic in May 2012.

ADAM DRURY

DATE OF BIRTH:	August 29, 1978
PLACE OF BIRTH:	Cottenham, Cambridgeshire
NATIONALITY:	English
NORWICH CITY APPEARANCES:	361
NORWICH CITY GOALS:	4
NORWICH CITY DEBUT:	March 31, 2001

Norwich City 2 Grimsby Town 1 (Nationwide Division One)

GRANT HANLEY

DATE OF BIRTH:	November 20, 1991
PLACE OF BIRTH:	Dumfries, Scotland
NATIONALITY:	Scottish
NORWICH CITY APPEARANCES:	183*
NORWICH CITY GOALS:	6*
NORWICH CITY DEBUT:	September 9, 2017

Norwich City 1 Birmingham City 0 (Championship)

*AS AT THE END OF THE 2022/23 SEASON

Grant Hanley has enjoyed two Championship title-winning season's as Norwich City captain.

The Scotland international defender has been a rock at the heart of the Norwich City defence since joining the Canaries in August 2017. Signed from Newcastle United, Hanley had previously made his name with Blackburn Rovers as a committed defender and team leader.

The City skipper is now the longest serving member of the current squad and a highly-respected character in the dressing room. Now approaching 200 games for Norwich City, Hanley will be keen to return to fitness and hit that double century landmark in 2024.

9

JOSH
SARGENT

FOOTY

ALL OF THESE FOOTY PHRASES
ARE HIDDEN IN THE GRID,
EXCEPT FOR ONE... BUT CAN YOU
WORK OUT WHICH ONE?

PHRASES

```
C A E S W Y V Y B H U G N U R Y M M U D
V U Q I D E R B Y D A Y O L U R T S S U
K F A D J L G T X T F C B E I A K C F P
I B H E O T L P Z R V N M W O J I R Y A
C M O F F S I D E R U L E E D S P E Y H
M E R U E I J R D E D A Q G S H L A X C
R X E R N H A T T R I C K O I L A M R T
E I Y O W W S L S N O W R S O Z Y E Y A
D C A A Z L W S J K T K Y V K B M R T M
A A L P X A U Y H M I D F I E D A R O E
E N P T K N F W G C P L J K A M K N L H
H W E J A I L O K H A O F O H I E C G T
G A M E O F T W O H A L V E S T R N U F
N V A I A H E S L F J D U A O I U O T O
I E G B I C L A S S A C T U P F G E V N
V D G O A E E U C K S S C Y W U L Q L A
I R I R Q G M N S A C H G H D O S F G M
D V B A C K O F T H E N E T Z P X B N A
```

Back of the Net

Big Game Player

Brace

Class Act

Derby Day

Diving Header

Dugout

Dummy Run

Final Whistle

Game of Two Halves

Half Volley

Hat-trick

Keepie Uppie

Man of the Match

Mexican Wave

Offside Rule

One-touch

Playmaker

Scissor Kick

Screamer

29

PLAYER

OF THE SEASON

BRAZILIAN MIDFIELDER GABRIEL SARA CAPPED OFF AN IMPRESSIVE DEBUT SEASON WITH THE CANARIES BY COLLECTING THE BARRY BUTLER MEMORIAL TROPHY AFTER SUPPORTERS VOTED HIM THE CLUB'S PLAYER OF THE SEASON FOR 2022/23.

The 23-year-old made 43 appearances in all competitions last season following his summer switch from Sao Paulo and fired home seven Championship goals. He was on target with memorable strikes in the Canaries' impressive victories away to play-off chasing Millwall and Blackburn Rovers in the final third of the season.

The all-action Brazilian was presented with the award at City's final home game of the season against Blackpool after he edged past runner-up Kenny McLean and third-placed Max Aarons following the annual supporters' poll.

After securing the accolade, Sara said: "I'm really happy with this. I wasn't expecting it, I had a tough start in Norwich but now I'm feeling good and I'm really, really happy with being the Player of the Season.

"I want to say thank you to everyone that voted for me, I'm very happy with it. It's really special to be chosen by the fans, they always support us and they are very special to me. This now makes them even more special to me.

YOUNG PLAYER OF THE SEASON

Liam Gibbs was crowned Norwich City's Young Player of the Season for 2022/23 following his breakthrough campaign at Carrow Road.

The midfielder, who joined the club from local rivals Ipswich Town in 2021, made 34 Championship appearances in 2022/23 after being handed his City debut by former head coach Dean Smith on the opening day of the season against Cardiff City.

Despite only turning 20 in December 2022, Gibbs produced a number of cultured and mature displays in the Canary midfield and netted his first goal in yellow and green in the 2-0 victory away to Blackburn Rovers on Good Friday.

"I'm absolutely delighted to have won," said Gibbs after being presented with the Etty Smith award. "I know that there are some big names who are now in the first team who have won this award in previous years, so I am hoping to follow in their footsteps and become a regular first-team player next season."

"It's been really positive since I joined the club. I had my first season in the under-23s and then managed to get a few appearances on the bench. I made my debut this season and kicked on really to have my first season in the first team. To win Young Player of the Season in your first season is really impressive so I'm really proud."

"I came and I had my injury, and everything for me was new; the language, the food, the weather. Everything was new for me, and the beginning was tough, really tough. The football is quite different as well. "Now, after a year, I feel really part of Norwich and really part of this team."

GABRIEL SARA

LIAM GIBBS

GABRIEL SARA

THE WALL PASS

With teams being very organised in modern football, it can be very difficult to break them down and create scoring opportunities. One of the best ways to achieve this is by using the 'wall pass', otherwise known as the quick one-two.

EXERCISE

In a non-pressurised situation, involving four players, A carries the ball forward towards a static defender (in this case a cone) and before reaching the defender, plays the ball to B before running around the opposite side to receive the one-touch return pass. A then delivers the ball safely to C who then repeats the exercise returning the ball to D, and in this way the exercise continues. Eventually a defender can be used to make the exercise more challenging, with all players being rotated every few minutes.

The exercise can progress into a five-a-side game, the diagram below shows how additional players (W) on the touchline can be used as 'walls' with just one touch available to help the man in possession of the ball.

Each touchline player can move up and down the touchline, but not enter the pitch - they can also play for either team.

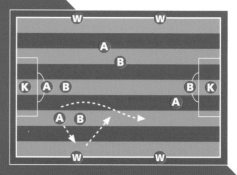

KEY FACTORS

1. Look to commit the defender before passing - do not play the ball too early.
2. Pass the ball firmly and to feet.
3. Accelerate past defender after passing.
4. Receiver (B) make themselves available for the pass.
5. B delivers a return pass, weighted correctly, into space.

SOCCER SKILLS

If done correctly, this is a tactic which is extremely difficult to stop, but needs teamwork and communication between the two attacking players.

ONEL
HERNÁNDEZ
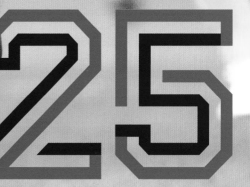

A-Z

ARE YOU READY TO TACKLE OUR A-Z FOOTBALL QUIZ?

THE SIMPLE RULE IS THAT THE ANSWERS RUN THROUGH THE 26 LETTERS OF THE ALPHABET.

A

What nationality is Watford goalkeeper Daniel Bachmann?

A _____

B

Which team won the Sky Bet Championship title in 2022/23?

B _____

C

Which Premier League club reappointed their former manager as interim boss in March 2023?

C _____

D

Which League One side play their home matches at Pride Park?

D _____

E

What nationality is Liverpool's sensational striker Mohamed Salah?

E _____

F

Which country knocked England out of the FIFA World Cup finals in 2022?

F _____

Which famous football ground is due to host its final fixture in 2024?

G

What is the name of Premier League new boys Luton Town's home ground?

K

Can you name the League One club that play their home matches at Brisbane Road?

L

H **Which club did Neil Warnock lead to Championship survival in 2022/23?**

H

Which Championship club boasted the division's top scorer in 2022/23?

M

I **Which country did England defeat 6–2 in their opening game of the FIFA 2022 World Cup finals?**

I

J **Aston Villa winger Leon Bailey plays internationally for which country?**

J

Q Can you name the country that hosted the FIFA 2022 World Cup finals?

Q _____

R Which Spanish side did Manchester City defeat in last season's UEFA Champions League semi-final?

R _____

S Which team knocked Premier League champions Manchester City out of the Carabao Cup last season?

S _____

T Which full-back left Huddersfield Town to join Nottingham Forest ahead of their return to the Premier League in the summer of 2022?

T _____

N

What nationality is Manchester City's ace marksman Erling Haaland?

N _____

O Can you name the former Premier League team that will compete in the National League in 2023/24?

O _____

P Which international striker ended five seasons with Norwich City in May 2023?

P _____

X Can you name the Portuguese international defender who played in the Premier League with Everton, Liverpool & Middlesbrough?

X _____

Y At which club did Leeds United's Luke Ayling make his league debut?

Y _____

Z Which Dutch international midfielder played Premier League football for Chelsea, Middlesbrough and Liverpool in the 2000s?

Z _____

U Can you name Brighton's German forward who joined the Seagulls in January 2022?

U _____

V Can you name the former England striker who has hit over 100 Premier League goals for Leicester City?

V _____

W Can you name the goalkeeper who scored a late equaliser at Blackburn Rovers last season in the Championship?

W _____

A-Z

PART TWO

ANSWERS ON PAGE 62

ASHLEY

BARNES

DESIGN A
FOOTY BOOT

Design a brilliant new footy boot
for the Canaries squad!

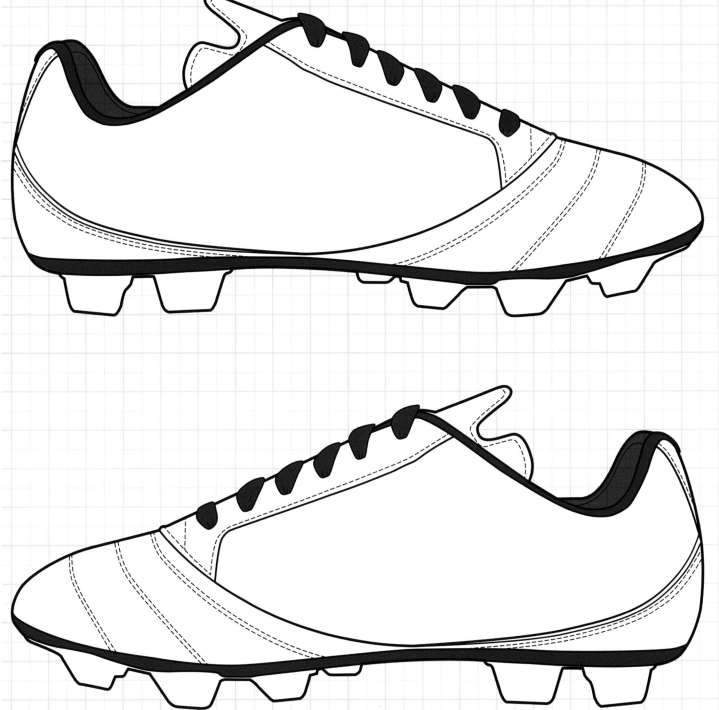

MIDFIELD
MAESTROS

WES HOOLAHAN, JAMES MADDISON AND EMI BUENDIA WERE ALL REAL CREATORS IN THE CANARY MIDFIELD. CONTINUING THAT FINE TRADITION IS CITY'S CHILEAN MAGICIAN MARCELINO NÚÑEZ.

James Maddison is an immensely talented midfielder who arrived at Carrow Road from Coventry City in January 2016.

After loan spells back with the Sky Blues and then north of the border with Aberdeen, he became a real class act in the Norwich City midfield. In 2017/18 Maddison emerged as the team's standout performer and ended the campaign as Norwich's top scorer with 15 goals and was awarded the Barry Butler Memorial Trophy as City's Player of the Season.

His performances for the Canaries won him a big money move to the Premier League with Leicester City and full international honours with England.

Wes Hoolahan was a wonderful Norwich City servant who enjoyed many ups and downs in a Canary career that experienced three promotions and three relegations.

He was initially recruited by Glenn Roeder from Blackpool back in 2008 and made a further 42 international appearances during his Carrow Road career. A supremely creative player, Hoolahan starred under Paul Lambert as City won back-to-back promotions to reach the Premier League. He was also a member of the 2014/15 play-off winning team that defeated Middlesbrough at Wembley.

His 10-year Carrow Road career concluded with the popular Irishman on target in a 2-1 victory over Leeds United in April 2018.

WES HOOLAHAN

DATE OF BIRTH: May 20, 1982

PLACE OF BIRTH: Dublin, Ireland

NATIONALITY: Irish

NORWICH CITY APPEARANCES: 352

NORWICH CITY GOALS: 54

NORWICH CITY DEBUT: August 9, 2008
Coventry City 2 Norwich City 0 (Championship)

JAMES MADDISON

DATE OF BIRTH: November 23, 1996

PLACE OF BIRTH: Coventry

NATIONALITY: English

NORWICH CITY APPEARANCES: 53

NORWICH CITY GOALS: 16

NORWICH CITY DEBUT: August 23, 2016
Norwich City 6 Coventry City 1 (League Cup)

Emi Buendia was a talented playmaker who was signed from Spanish side Getafe in the summer of 2018.

The diminutive Argentinean was a star performer as Norwich won the 2018/19 Championship title. Buendia's performances were one of very few bright spots in the Canaries' 2019/20 Premier League campaign and in 2020/21 he proved to be a cut above anything the Championship had to offer as he shone in the Canaries latest promotion.

With 15 league goals and countless assists – mainly for Teemu Pukki, Buendia ended 2020/21 as the EFL Player of the Season and Norwich's Player of the Season too. His 2020/21 displays have seen him regarded by many City fans as one of the club's greatest-ever players.

EMI BUENDIA

DATE OF BIRTH: December 25, 1996

PLACE OF BIRTH: Mar del Plata, Argentina

NATIONALITY: Argentinean

NORWICH CITY APPEARANCES: 121

NORWICH CITY GOALS: 24

NORWICH CITY DEBUT: August 25, 2018
Norwich City 0 Leeds United 3 (Championship)

MARCELINO NÚÑEZ

DATE OF BIRTH: March 1, 2000

PLACE OF BIRTH: Recoleta, Santiago, Chile

NATIONALITY: Chilean

NORWICH CITY APPEARANCES: 39*

NORWICH CITY GOALS: 3*

NORWICH CITY DEBUT: August 6, 2022
Norwich City 1 Wigan Athletic 1 (Championship)

*AS AT THE END OF THE 2022/23 SEASON

Marcelino Núñez joined Norwich City at the start of their 2022/23 Sky Bet Championship campaign after signing from Universidad Catolica.

Comfortable in possession and always looking to create an attacking opportunity for the team, Núñez made a great impression in his debut campaign as a Canary.

A full Chilean international, Núñez bagged his first goal for the Canaries with a stunning free-kick away to Hull City and later in the season he netted the club's Goal of the Season with his sensational strike against Birmingham City at Carrow Road. With the benefit of a season's experience in the English game now under his belt, great things will be anticipated from Núñez in 2023/24.

CLASSIC FAN'TASTIC

Captain Canary is hiding in the crowd in five different places as Norwich City fans celebrate promotion to the Premier League in 2011. **Can you find all five?** ANSWERS ON PAGE 62

JONATHAN
ROWE
27

GOAL
OF THE SEASON

CHILEAN INTERNATIONAL MIDFIELDER MARCELINO NÚÑEZ MARKED A TWO-GOAL MAN OF THE MATCH PERFORMANCE WITH NORWICH CITY'S GOAL OF THE SEASON FOR 2022/23 WHEN HE OPENED THE SCORING IN THE CANARIES' 3-1 VICTORY OVER BIRMINGHAM CITY IN FEBRUARY 2023.

Núñez netted twice in the space of 10 first-half minutes to give the home side a 2-0 lead at the break. However, it was his opening goal that will be talked about for many years to come. The 23-year-old's superb strike came after 27 minutes following a Norwich corner.

The initial corner kick had been headed away by Blues' defender Kevin Long but fell to Núñez some two yards outside the penalty area.

From the moment the ball left Núñez's boot there was only one place it was going and once the ball hit the back of net that was City's goal of the season contest decided in an instant.

To strike the ball with great power and accuracy from such a distance showed exceptional technique and the goal was met with a seal of appreciation and approval from the Carrow Road faithful.

Clearly brimming with supreme confidence after scoring such a wonder-goal, Núñez made it 2-0 on 36-minutes when he met Kenny McLean's smart ball from the left with another right-foot finish at the River End.

After the break Núñez turned from scorer to provider when he teed up Christos Tzolis for the Canaries' third and final goal of the night to secure a 3-1 win under the lights on home soil.

While Núñez goal was the standout strike of 2022/23 other notable Canary goals were scored by player of the season Gabriel Sara against Millwall and Blackburn Rovers. While Birmingham City were once again on the receiving end when Jacob Sørensen fired home an impressive effort from distance in the League Cup victory over Blues at Carrow Road in August 2022.

After the opposition failed to close him down Núñez connected with a tremendous right-foot volley which dipped into the bottom left corner – with former Canary 'keeper John Ruddy a mere bystander in the visitors' goal.

MARCELINO NÚÑEZ

BEHIND THE

BADGE

...HIDDEN BEHIND OUR BEAUTIFUL BADGE?

A

C

B

D

E

G

F

H

49

17

GABRIEL
SARA

TRUE COLOURS

HAVE FUN COLOURING IN THIS PICTURE OF CANARIES STAR

GABRIEL SARA

51

STUNNING STRIKERS

IWAN ROBERTS, GRANT HOLT AND TEEMU PUKKI WERE ALL ACE MARKSMEN FOR NORWICH CITY. LOOKING TO FOLLOW IN THEIR FOOTSTEPS IS AMERICAN INTERNATIONAL JOSH SARGENT.

Grant Holt became a goalscoring legend at Carrow Road who was adored by the Norwich fans during four memorable seasons at the Club.

Signed by Bryan Gunn from Shrewsbury Town in 2009, he flourished under Paul Lambert who also made him City captain. Top scorer as City won the League One title in 2009/10, he netted a memorable hat-trick against Ipswich Town en route to promotion from the Championship in 2010/11 which further enhanced his reputation with the fans.

Holt then took the Premier League by storm in 2011/12 as City comfortably maintained their top-flight status. He is the only player to win the club's Player of the Season accolade on three occasions.

Iwan Roberts scored an impressive 96 goals for the Canaries between 1997 and 2004. He was signed by Mike Walker from Wolves for a fee of £850,000 in the summer of 1997.

Despite a disappointing first season in Norfolk, Roberts went on to become one of the Carrow Road crowd's all-time favourite players.

He was twice voted Player of the Season and won a place in the inaugural Hall of Fame during the Centenary celebrations. Roberts captained City in their 2001/02 play-off final against Birmingham in the Millennium Stadium and also chipped in with vital goals during the 2003/04 Nationwide First Division title-winning campaign.

IWAN ROBERTS

DATE OF BIRTH: June 26, 1968

PLACE OF BIRTH: Bangor, Wales

NATIONALITY: Welsh

NORWICH CITY APPEARANCES: 306

NORWICH CITY GOALS: 96

NORWICH CITY DEBUT: August 9, 1997
Norwich City 0 Wolves 2 (Nationwide Division One)

GRANT HOLT

DATE OF BIRTH: April 12, 1981

PLACE OF BIRTH: Carlisle

NATIONALITY: English

NORWICH CITY APPEARANCES: 168

NORWICH CITY GOALS: 78

NORWICH CITY DEBUT: August 8, 2009
Norwich City 1 Colchester United 7 (League One)

Teemu Pukki Finnish striker Teemu Pukki netted 88 goals in his five seasons at Norwich City and ended his Canary career as the club's fourth highest goalscorer.

Forming a great on-pitch understanding with Emi Buendia, Pukki was twice a Championship title winner with the Canaries. He bagged a Premier League hat-trick against Newcastle United in 2019 and also became his country's all-time leading goalscorer while a Norwich City player.

Having joined Norwich City initially on a free transfer from Bromdby, the Fin is widely regarded as being the club best-ever 'free transfer'.

Twice voted Player of the Season at Carrow Road, Pukki left Norwich at the end of last season.

TEEMU PUKKI

DATE OF BIRTH: March 29, 1990

PLACE OF BIRTH: Kolta, Finland

NATIONALITY: Finnish

NORWICH CITY APPEARANCES: 210

NORWICH CITY GOALS: 88

NORWICH CITY DEBUT: August 4, 2018
Birmingham City 2 Norwich City 2 (Championship)

JOSH SARGENT

DATE OF BIRTH: February 20, 2000

PLACE OF BIRTH: Missouri, USA

NATIONALITY: American

NORWICH CITY APPEARANCES: 70*

NORWICH CITY GOALS: 17*

NORWICH CITY DEBUT: August 14, 2021
Norwich City 0 Liverpool 3 (Premier League)

*AS AT THE END OF THE 2022/23 SEASON

JOSH SARGENT enjoyed a positive 2022/23 season at Carrow Road and ended the campaign as the club's leading scorer with 13 Championship goals to his name.

The hard-working American international forward made an impressive start to last season with four goals in August as City recorded victories over Huddersfield Town, Millwall and Sunderland. His impressive form continued across the first half of the campaign and was rewarded with a place in the USA's World Cup finals squad for Qatar 2022.

With the ability to play through the middle as an out-and-out striker, or in an attacking role on either flank, a great deal will be expected of Sargent in 2023/24.

REWIND

Preston North End 0
Norwich City 4

SKY BET CHAMPIONSHIP · JANUARY 14, 2023

Norwich City made a flying start to life under new head coach David Wagner as the Canaries marked his first league game in charge with an impressive 4-0 win away to Preston North End.

Teemu Pukki opened the scoring after just 13 minutes and Kieran Dowell added a first-half brace to put City firmly in the driving seat at half-time.

Pukki's second goal of the game 21 minutes from time wrapped up what was the team's most comprehensive result of the season.

Millwall 2
Norwich City 3

SKY BET CHAMPIONSHIP · MARCH 4, 2023

The Canaries recorded a third consecutive Championship triumph when they won a thrilling match away to Millwall in March 2023.

Although the Lions took a 20th-minute lead, Norwich levelled before half-time when Jacob Sørensen netted following a smartly worked set-piece. Second-half pressure led to Tom Bradshaw scoring an own-goal to put Norwich 2-1 up before Gabriel Sara netted a stunning third. The host's reduced the arrears seven minutes from the end but Norwich held firm for the win.

Blackburn Rovers 0
Norwich City 2

SKY BET CHAMPIONSHIP · APRIL 7, 2023

Norwich gained a level of revenge over Blackburn Rovers for a league defeat and an FA Cup exit at Carrow Road when David Wagner's men began their Easter schedule with an excellent 2-0 victory at Ewood Park.

A superb strike from Liam Gibbs gave Norwich City an 11th-minute lead and from that moment on the Canaries never looked back. The perfect away performance was secured by City's second goal which came thanks to another stunning effort from Gabriel Sara.

FAST FORWARD

THREE BIG CHAMPIONSHIP ENCOUNTERS TO COME IN 2024...

Southampton (HOME)

SKY BET CHAMPIONSHIP · JANUARY 1, 2024

The calendar year of 2024 begins with a New Year's Day visit from former Premier League side Southampton. That in-turn means there will be a familiar face in the opposition dugout with former Carrow Road favourite Russell Martin now the Saints' head coach.

Martin made 309 appearances for Norwich City and captained the club to victory in the 2015 play-off final at Wembley. He has emerged as one of the game's brightest young coaches having previously been in charge of MK Dons and Swansea City.

Against a team relegated from the top-flight last season, the match is sure to provide a stern test for the Canaries.

Leeds United (AWAY)

SKY BET CHAMPIONSHIP · JANUARY 27, 2024

The month of January concludes with another match against one of last season's relegated teams and another Canary reunion too.

Now under the guidance of former City head coach Daniel Farke, Leeds United will be among the favourites to secure an instant return to the top flight. Having led the Canaries to two Championship titles while at Carrow Road, welcoming his former side to Elland Road is likely to be an emotional occasion for the popular German coach.

Matches against the West Yorkshire side have certainly been both eventful and important in recent seasons and this latest clash at Elland Road is sure to be no different.

Ipswich Town (HOME)

SKY BET CHAMPIONSHIP · APRIL 6, 2024

Having spent the last four seasons down in the third tier of English football, local rivals Ipswich Town capitalised on a surprise end-of-season slump from Sheffield Wednesday to squeak promotion in 2022/23.

The Blues' return to the Championship of course reinstates the East Anglian derby fixture and that means local bragging rights will be at stake once again this season.

Prior to the current season, Norwich City have enjoyed a decade of dominance in East Anglia and are unbeaten against Town since April 2009. The Blues have not won a league match at Carrow Road since February 2006.

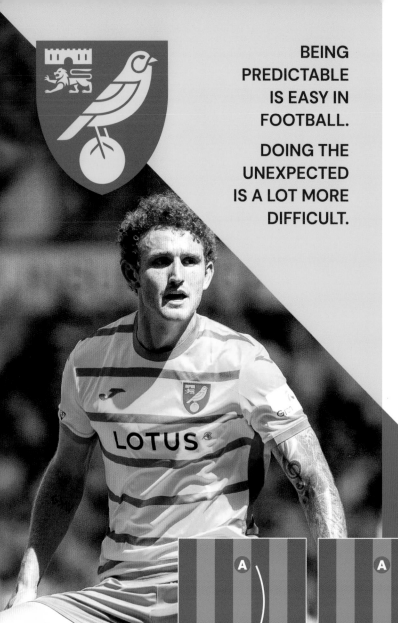

BEING PREDICTABLE IS EASY IN FOOTBALL.

DOING THE UNEXPECTED IS A LOT MORE DIFFICULT.

TURNING WITH THE BALL

One of the biggest problems a defence can have to deal with is when a skilful player is prepared to turn with the ball and run at them, committing a key defender into making a challenge. Because football today is so fast and space so precious, this is becoming a rare skill.

EXERCISE

In an area 20m x 10m, A plays the ball into B who turns, and with two touches maximum plays the ball into C. C controls and reverses the process. After a few minutes the middleman is changed.

As you progress, a defender is brought in to oppose B, and is initially encouraged to play a 'passive' role. B has to turn and play the ball to C who is allowed to move along the baseline.

The type of turns can vary. Players should be encouraged to use the outside of the foot, inside of the foot, with feint and disguise to make space for the turn.

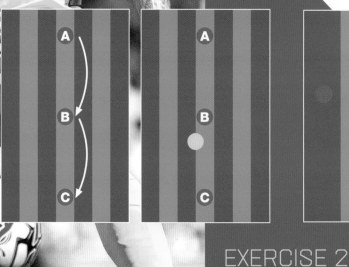

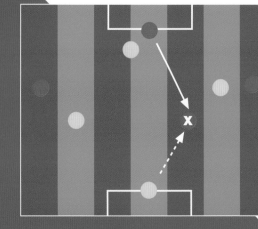

EXERCISE 2

As the players grow in confidence, you can move forward to a small-sided game. In this example of a 4-a-side practice match, X has made space for himself to turn with the ball, by coming off his defender at an angle. By doing this he can see that the defender has not tracked him, and therefore has the awareness to turn and attack.

SOCCER SKILLS

Matches at the top level are won and lost by pieces of skill such as this, so players have to be brave enough to go in search of the ball, and turn in tight situations.

DIMITRIS
GIANNOULIS

30

TEST YOUR CANARIES KNOWLEDGE & MEMORY WITH OUR HIGH FIVES QUIZ

HIGH FIVES

1. Who are Norwich City's all-time top five record goalscorers?

1.

2.

3.

4.

5.

2. Can you name the Club's all-time top five appearance makers?

1.

2.

3.

4.

5.

3. Prior to David Wagner, who were City's last five permanent managers?

1.

2.

3.

4.

5.

4. Can you name Norwich City's last five FA Cup opponents?

1.

2.

3.

4.

5.

5. Can you name the Canaries' final league position from each of the last five seasons?

1. _____
2. _____
3. _____
4. _____
5. _____

8. Can you recall the last five seasons that Norwich City competed in the Premier League?

1. _____
2. _____
3. _____
4. _____
5. _____

6. Which members of the City squad started the most Championship games last season?

1. _____
2. _____
3. _____
4. _____
5. _____

9. Can you recall the Canaries' last five Championship victories from last season?

1. _____
2. _____
3. _____
4. _____
5. _____

7. Who were the Canaries' top five Championship goalscorers last season?

1. _____
2. _____
3. _____
4. _____
5. _____

10. Can you recall the last five seasons when Norwich City have been league champions?

1. _____
2. _____
3. _____
4. _____
5. _____

SENSATIONAL STOPPERS

BRYAN GUNN, ROBERT GREEN AND JOHN RUDDY WERE ALL GREAT CANARY 'KEEPERS. CONTINUING THAT PROUD TREND IS CURRENT CITY STOPPER ANGUS GUNN.

Robert Green became the sixth Norwich City player to be capped for England when he appeared as a substitute against Colombia in the United States in June 2005.

He had previously progressed through the youth and reserve ranks at Carrow Road and played a key role in Norwich reaching the 2001/02 play-off final. The young 'keeper then enjoyed an exceptional season in 2003/04 when the Canaries were crowned Nationwide First Division champions.

As a City player, Green was named as one of three 'keepers in the final England 2006 World Cup squad only for injury to prevent him from travelling to Germany for the finals.

Bryan Gunn arrived at Carrow Road in October 1986 following a £100,000 transfer from Aberdeen. Over the next 12 years he amassed 477 appearances for the club and became one of the most popular players to ever play for Norwich City.

An outstanding shot-stopper, Gunn controlled his area with authority and was also comfortable with the ball at his feet. His performances twice saw him win the Barry Butler Memorial Trophy as the club's Player of the Season.

A key performer in Mike Walker's 1992/93 side that battled for the Premier League title - Gunn played in all six of the club's UEFA Cup fixtures the following season.

BRYAN GUNN

DATE OF BIRTH: December 22, 1963

PLACE OF BIRTH: Thurso, Scotland

NATIONALITY: Scottish

NORWICH CITY APPEARANCES: 477

NORWICH CITY DEBUT: November 4, 1986
Norwich City 2 Coventry City 1 (Full Members Cup)

ROBERT GREEN

DATE OF BIRTH: January 18, 1980

PLACE OF BIRTH: Chertsey, Surrey

NATIONALITY: English

NORWICH CITY APPEARANCES: 241

NORWICH CITY DEBUT: April 11, 1999
Norwich City 0 Ipswich Town 0 (Nationwide Division One)

John Ruddy won an England cap and two promotions to the top flight during a superb seven-year stint at Carrow Road.

Signed by Paul Lambert from Everton in the summer of 2010, the former Cambridge United 'keeper was part of the club's 2010/11 promotion-winning side that went on to feature in the Premier League for the next three seasons.

The long-serving goalkeeper was also a member of City's 2014/15 play-off side that enjoyed semi-final success over arch-rivals Ipswich Town before gaining promotion with victory over Middlesbrough in the Wembley final. For the majority of his time with the Canaries, Ruddy was first choice goalkeeper unless injury dictated otherwise.

JOHN RUDDY

DATE OF BIRTH: October 24, 1986

PLACE OF BIRTH: St Ives, Cambridgeshire

NATIONALITY: English

NORWICH CITY APPEARANCES: 243

NORWICH CITY DEBUT: August 6, 2010
Norwich City 3 Watford 3 (Championship)

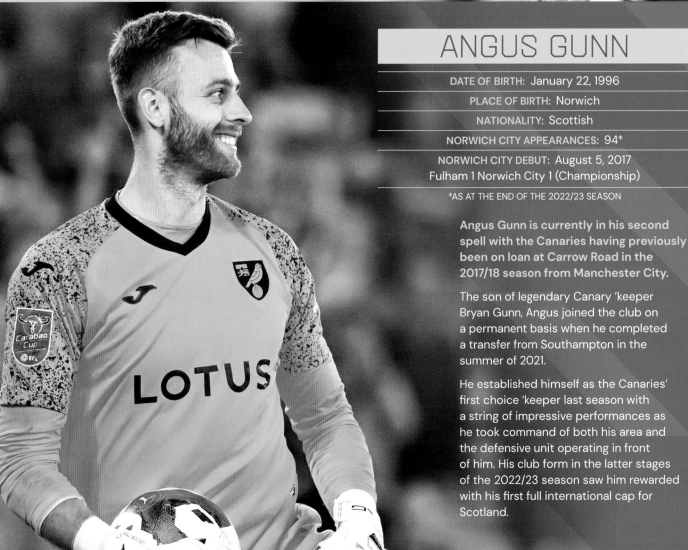

ANGUS GUNN

DATE OF BIRTH: January 22, 1996

PLACE OF BIRTH: Norwich

NATIONALITY: Scottish

NORWICH CITY APPEARANCES: 94*

NORWICH CITY DEBUT: August 5, 2017
Fulham 1 Norwich City 1 (Championship)

*AS AT THE END OF THE 2022/23 SEASON

Angus Gunn is currently in his second spell with the Canaries having previously been on loan at Carrow Road in the 2017/18 season from Manchester City.

The son of legendary Canary 'keeper Bryan Gunn, Angus joined the club on a permanent basis when he completed a transfer from Southampton in the summer of 2021.

He established himself as the Canaries' first choice 'keeper last season with a string of impressive performances as he took command of both his area and the defensive unit operating in front of him. His club form in the latter stages of the 2022/23 season saw him rewarded with his first full international cap for Scotland.

ANSWERS

PAGE 29: FOOTY PHRASES

Keepie Uppie.

PAGE 34: A–Z QUIZ

A. Austrian. B. Burnley. C. Crystal Palace. D. Derby County. E. Egyptian. F. France. G. Goodison Park (Everton). H. Huddersfield Town. I. Iran. J. Jamaica. K. Kenilworth Road. L. Leyton Orient. M. Middlesbrough (Chuba Akpom). N. Norwegian. O. Oldham Athletic. P. Pukki, Teemu. Q. Qatar. R. Real Madrid. S. Southampton. T. Toffolo, Harry. U. Undav, Deniz. V. Vardy, Jamie. W. Wilson, Ben (Coventry City). X. Xavier, Abel. Y. Yeovil Town. Z. Zenden, Boudewijn.

PAGE 21: SPOT THE DIFFERENCE

PAGE 42: FAN'TASTIC

PAGE 48: BEHIND THE BADGE

A. Christian Fassnacht. B. Dimitris Giannoulis. C. Ashley Barnes. D. Josh Sargent. E. Marcelino Núñez. F. Tony Springett. G. Jack Stacey. H. Shane Duffy.

PAGE 58: HIGH FIVES

QUIZ 1:
1. Johnny Gavin (132 goals).
2. Terry Allcock (127 goals).
3. Iwan Roberts (96 goals).
4. Teemu Pukki (88 goals).
5. Jack Vinall (80 goals).

QUIZ 2:
1. Kevin Keelan (673 appearances).
2. Ron Ashman (662 appearances).
3. Dave Stringer (499 appearances).
4. Bryan Gunn (477 appearances).
5. Joe Hannah (427 appearances).

QUIZ 3:
1. Dean Smith. 2. Daniel Farke. 3. Alex Neil. 4. Neil Adams. 5. Chris Hughton.

QUIZ 4:
1. Blackburn Rovers (2022/23). 2. Liverpool (2021/22). 3. Wolverhampton Wanderers (2021/22). 4. Charlton Athletic (2021/22). 5. Barnsley (2020/21).

QUIZ 5:
1. 13th in the Championship (2022/23). 2. 20th in the Premier League (2021/22). 3. 1st in the Championship (2020/21). 4. 20th in the Premier League (2019/20). 5. 1st in the Championship (2018/19).

QUIZ 6:
1. Max Aarons (44 Championship starts). 2. Grant Hanley (39 Championship starts). 3. Josh Sargent (37 Championship starts). 4. Kenny McLean (34 Championship starts). 5. Teemu Pukki (33 Championship starts).

QUIZ 7:
1. Josh Sargent (13 goals). 2. Teemu Pukki (10 goals). 3. Gabriel Sara (7 goals). 4. Kieran Dowell (5 goals). 5. Marcelino Núñez (3 goals).

QUIZ 8:
1. 2021/22. 2. 2019/20. 3. 2015/16. 4. 2013/14. 5. 2012/13

QUIZ 9:
1. Blackburn Rovers (A) 2-0, April 7, 2023.
2. Millwall (A) 3-2, March 4, 2023.
3. Cardiff City (H) 2-0, February 25, 2023
4. Birmingham City (H) 2-0, February 21, 2023
5. Hull City (H) 3-1, February 14, 2023

QUIZ 10:
1. 2022/21 (Second tier champions). 2. 2018/19 (Second tier champions) 3. 2009/10 (Third tier champions). 4. 2003/04 (Second tier champions). 5. 1985/96 (Second tier champions).